THE RISKS OF
FENTANYL AND
OTHER OPIOIDS

Peggy J. Parks

ReferencePoint
Press

San Diego, CA

© 2021 ReferencePoint Press, Inc.
Printed in the United States

For more information, contact:
ReferencePoint Press, Inc.
PO Box 27779
San Diego, CA 92198
www.ReferencePointPress.com

LIBRARY OF CONGRESS CATALOGING-IN-PUBLICATION DATA

Names: Parks, Peggy J., 1951- author.
Title: The risks of fentanyl and other opioids / by Peggy J. Parks.
Description: San Diego, CA : ReferencePoint Press, 2021. | Series: Drug
  risks | Includes bibliographical references and index.
Identifiers: LCCN 2020000104 (print) | LCCN 2020000105 (ebook) | ISBN
  9781682829110 (library binding) | ISBN 9781682829127 (ebook)
Subjects: LCSH: Opioid abuse--United States. | Opioids--Therapeutic
  use--United States.
Classification: LCC RC568.O45 P37 2021 (print) | LCC RC568.O45 (ebook) |
  DDC 362.29/30973--dc23
LC record available at https://lccn.loc.gov/2020000104
LC ebook record available at https://lccn.loc.gov/2020000105

CONTENTS

When Medicine Kills

What Are Opioids?

Opioids are drugs that relieve pain by dulling the senses. Natural opioids like opium and morphine come from poppy plants that are grown mostly in Southeast Asia, Southwest Asia, and Mexico. Heroin is a derivative of morphine. Semisynthetic opioids like the painkilling drugs OxyContin, Vicodin, and Percocet are human-made but mimic the effects of natural opioids. Fentanyl is a purely synthetic opioid that is fifty to one hundred times more potent than other opioids—which makes it the deadliest of them all.

When people think about the most dangerous and addictive drugs, they may recall frightening news stories about heroin, methamphetamine, or newer drugs like K2, Spice, Molly, and bath salts. Of all the dangerous drugs that come to mind, medications prescribed by doctors are probably not what people think of first. But the reality is, prescription painkilling drugs known as opioids, including counterfeit versions of them, are killing more people than any other drugs that exist. This has created a full-blown health crisis in the United States—one that has led US health officials to declare a public health emergency.

An August 2019 report from the Centers for Disease Control and Prevention (CDC) shows that the number of overdose deaths involving opioids jumped from 25,052 in 2013 to 47,600 in 2017— a 90 percent increase in four years. The soaring prevalence of opioid-related overdose deaths is largely due to a spike in the use of fentanyl, a powerful synthetic opioid that is far more potent than all other opioids. According to Bloomberg School of Public Health researcher Carl Latkin, these statistics are appalling—but not really surprising. "Fentanyl is really a very nasty drug,"[1] he says.

Potent Painkillers

Opioids are drugs that relieve discomfort by blocking pain signals from the body to the brain. Some of the most widely prescribed opioids are OxyContin (oxycodone); Percocet (acetaminophen combined with oxycodone); Vicodin (hydrocodone combined with acetaminophen); and fentanyl. Heroin is also an opioid, but unlike the others, it is illegal, including for medical use.

Opioids were originally developed to provide pain relief for people suffering from advanced cancer or serious, debilitating injuries. Over time opioids' painkilling properties created a rising demand for the drugs—which in turn led to an exorbitant spike in the number of prescriptions doctors were writing. According to the CDC, American physicians wrote 191 million prescriptions for opioid painkillers in 2017. The actual amount of opioids in circulation is unknown, however, since these drugs are now being illicitly manufactured—but the number is believed to be astronomical.

Fentanyl has made the nationwide fight against opioid abuse an even tougher battle. Like other opioids, it was originally developed for legitimate medical use, although because of its potency it was prescribed sparingly and selectively. Fentanyl was used, for instance, as a surgical anesthetic or was prescribed for patients suffering from crippling pain at the end of their lives. According to surgeon Jedediah Kaufman, who has given fentanyl to his surgical patients, dose quantities are measured in micrograms—one-millionth of a gram. Fentanyl can slow or even stop breathing, so patients who take it are closely monitored by a physician.

Fentanyl that is illegally manufactured is often mixed in with street drugs such as cocaine, heroin, or methamphetamine. It is also mixed with other opioids, pressed into pills, and sold on the street or online by unscrupulous sellers on a hidden part of the internet known as the Dark Web.

Fentanyl-Related Deaths Soar

In August 2019, when the CDC released its report on opioid-related overdose deaths, there appeared to be some good news amid the bad. After a steady, steep rise in drug overdose deaths,

The powerful opioid known as fentanyl has made America's fight against opioid abuse tougher than ever. This bag contains more than 1 million fentanyl pills that were smuggled into the United States by drug cartels.

preliminary figures for 2018 showed a slight decrease of 5 percent. This was the first time since 1990 that drug-related deaths had declined, so health officials viewed it as a hopeful sign. But bad news overshadowed the positive finding. The report showed an enormous spike in fentanyl-related overdose deaths: nearly thirty-two thousand in one year alone. This was in sharp contrast to 2014, when the drug was much rarer and was detected in fewer than six thousand fatal overdoses. No drug in history has ever claimed as many lives in one year as has fentanyl.

Since the 2019 CDC report, the fentanyl crisis has shown no signs of slowing down. Many regions of the United States have seen continued spikes in overdose deaths involving fentanyl, including the Northeast, Midwest, and Pacific Northwest. In September 2019 three high school students from the Seattle, Washington, area died of fentanyl-related overdose within a few weeks of each other. One of the teens was Gabe Lilienthal, a seventeen-year-old who died after taking M30, a counterfeit OxyContin pill that was laced with fentanyl. People were shocked to hear that Lilienthal had overdosed, saying that taking drugs was completely out of character for him. He was a straight-A student. He was not much of a partier, loved sculpting, worked at a part-time job, and was learning to fly a plane. But he had been troubled by anxiety and insomnia, and his family believes he bought the pill to help him sleep.

Lilienthal's family is convinced that he had no idea the pill contained fentanyl. Kaufman, his stepfather, emphasizes how much more powerful fentanyl is than OxyContin or other opioids. "With fentanyl, it takes almost nothing to overdose," says Kaufman. "That's really why fentanyl is a death drug."[2]

A Nationwide Health Crisis

Because fentanyl has been detected in so many different drugs and plays a role in thousands of overdose deaths, it has led to a crisis. Physicians, public health officials, and those who work in law enforcement tend to share Kaufman's belief about his stepson's unawareness of fentanyl in the drug he bought. They are deeply concerned that drug users, including teenagers, are buying opioids laced with fentanyl and have no idea what they are putting into their bodies.

The soaring prevalence of fentanyl-related deaths is a major problem across the United States. And despite a small decline in overall drug overdose deaths during 2018, more than sixty-seven thousand people still died from drug overdoses that year—more than those who were killed in car crashes or died from gun violence. "Our nation's heroin and opioid crisis," says physician and public health researcher Daniel Cicca-rone, "has become more and more horrific."[3]

CHAPTER ONE

A Growing Health Crisis

The United States is in the grip of the deadliest drug-related crisis in the nation's history. According to the US Department of Health and Human Services, more than four hundred thousand people died of an opioid-related overdose from 1999 to 2017. Health officials say the rise in opioid abuse and opioid-related deaths happened in three distinct waves—but it all began with a massive increase in prescription opioid use.

The first wave, says physician and public health researcher Daniel Ciccarone, was the prescription painkiller epidemic, "in which powerful opioids were prescribed at alarming rates, causing mass dependency issues that continue today."[4] In 1990, opioid prescriptions in the United States totaled approximately 3 million. The number steadily increased each year, reaching 11 million by 1999. A catalyst for this growth was Purdue Pharma's introduction and aggressive marketing of OxyContin in the mid-1990s. Demand for the new drug, as well as other types of opioids, soared. According to the US Agency for Healthcare Research and Quality, by 2002 more than 85 million Americans were taking prescription opioids.

The second wave of the opioid epidemic began in 2010, with a huge spike in heroin addiction and overdose deaths. Many people who became addicted to opioids and were no longer able to get them turned to heroin because it was much cheaper and easier to buy on the street. By 2013 the third wave had begun with the arrival of new, frighteningly powerful synthetic opioids, including fentanyl.

Drugs from Poppy Plants

The biggest reason people seek out prescription opioids is that the drugs are effective at relieving pain. They are also known as narcotics, which comes from the Greek word *narke*, meaning "numbness" or "stupor." This is a fitting term, since opioids dull the senses, cause drowsiness, and relieve pain. Some opioids can also cause a sense of euphoria, which makes drug users want to keep taking them in order to recapture the feeling of being high.

The grandfather of opioids is opium, which comes from a poppy plant known as *Papaver somniferum*. Huge fields of these bright-red poppies grow in remote, mountainous countries that have warm, dry climates. According to the Drug Enforcement Administration (DEA), the primary poppy-growing region of the world is an area that stretches across central Asia from Turkey through Pakistan and Burma. Opium poppies are also grown in Latin America, notably Colombia and Mexico.

After the poppy blossoms drop off, globe-shaped seed pods are left behind. These pods are harvested for their milky sap, which contains raw opium. The opium can then be refined to extract morphine. What happens next depends on the intent — whether legal or illegal. For legal use, US government regulations oversee morphine production to ensure safety and purity. Morphine is a powerful painkiller and is often used in medical settings to treat patients who have undergone surgery or suffered a serious injury. Physicians may also prescribe morphine for people who are in the advanced stages of cancer or suffering from other serious illnesses that result in severe pain.

The Soaring Incidence of Opioid Overdose

US health officials refer to opioid abuse as a nationwide epidemic, and the exponential rise in overdose deaths is a strong indicator of why. In 1999, 8,050 people in the United States died of an overdose involving opioids, and by 2017 the number had risen to 47,600—an increase of 491 percent.

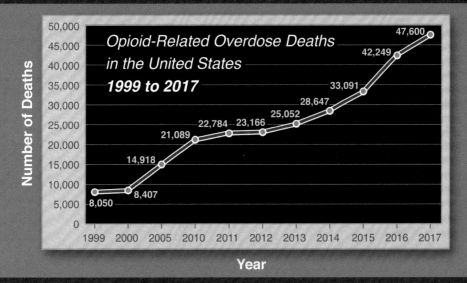

Opioid-Related Overdose Deaths in the United States 1999 to 2017

Source: Centers for Disease Control and Prevention, "Data Brief 329. Drug Overdose Deaths in the United States, 1999–2017," November 2019. www.cdc.gov.

Morphine is also used for illicit purposes. It may be sold for illegal nonmedical use or used to make heroin, a highly addictive drug that affects the brain faster than morphine does. Because heroin is illegal and its production therefore prohibited, the drug is produced in clandestine laboratories, such as those tucked away in remote areas of Mexico. But heroin has not always been illegal. In the 1890s scientists (mistakenly) concluded that heroin was safer and less addictive than morphine, and the German company Bayer began manufacturing it. The company added heroin to aspirin and marketed it as medicine for parents to give children who suffered from sore throats, coughs, and colds. "Some bottles depicted children eagerly reaching for the medicine, with moms giving their sick kids heroin on a spoon,"[5] says History.com writer Brynn Holland. By the early 1900s scientists realized how

A Warning Ignored

In August 2019 the news organization Politico obtained a confidential document that contained some troubling revelations. It was a March 2006 memo to the US surgeon general from National Institute on Drug Abuse director Nora Volkow. In the memo, Volkow warned about a dramatic rise in opioid addiction, including among teenagers. She urged the surgeon general to issue an official call to action, which is a powerful tool reserved for the most urgent circumstances. Volkow believed it was necessary in order to alert the public about what she perceived as an emerging health crisis.

But the call to action was never issued. Over the coming months, attention to the opioids problem dwindled as other issues took precedence. Although theories abound, no one knows for sure why. Perhaps health officials were consumed with other problems they believed to be more pressing, or perhaps they did not fully grasp the magnitude of the crisis—although they do now. John Walters, who was director of the White House Office of National Drug Control Policy at the time, cannot help wishing the surgeon general had issued the call to action as Volkow recommended. "Would it have ended the crisis? Probably not," says Walters. "But it would have increased awareness. More people would have known the dangers. We would have saved more lives."

Quoted in Brianna Ehley, "Federal Scientists Warned of Coming Opioid Crisis in 2006," Politico, August 21, 2019. www.politico.com.

erroneous their belief about heroin had been, and in 1924 the drug was banned by US law. It was too late to undo the damage, however. The widespread acceptance of heroin's medicinal use had resulted in a huge increase in people who had become addicted to the drug.

Although morphine and heroin are often called opioids, they are officially opiates, meaning drugs that are made from opium. Opioids mimic the effects of opiates but are partially or entirely synthetic, meaning human-made rather than made from natural plant derivatives. Despite these differences, the word *opioids* has become an umbrella term that is often used to refer to all narcotics, whether natural or synthetic.

The Rise of Semisynthetic Opioids

Semisynthetic opioids are not made from opium, but their chemical structures are similar to opiates. Some of the most well-known semisynthetic opioid brands include OxyContin, whose chemical name is oxycodone; Percocet, which is a combination of oxycodone and acetaminophen (the ingredient found in Tylenol); and Vicodin, which combines acetaminophen with an opioid called hydrocodone.

Percocet and Vicodin were introduced in the mid- to late 1970s. Doctors remained skeptical about prescribing highly addictive opioids to patients, but that perspective began to change in the 1980s. A January 1980 letter to the editor published in the *New England Journal of Medicine* challenged the long-accepted practice of using opioids only for patients suffering from the most severe pain, like from cancer. The letter, which was written by physicians, said that according to their own study of 11,882 patients whom they had treated with opioids, only 4 patients became addicted. The doctors wrote, "We conclude that despite widespread use of narcotic drugs in hospitals, the development of addiction is rare in medical patients with no history of addiction."[6] That endorsement cleared the way for widespread advocacy of opioid painkillers. Before long, the drugs were being prolifically prescribed for all kinds of pain.

Synthetic Opioids

Like semisynthetic opioids, synthetic opioids have a chemical makeup that is similar to natural opiates, but they are entirely human-made. Methadone is one example of a synthetic opioid. It is often used to treat recovering heroin addicts because it reduces withdrawal symptoms without causing the high of heroin. Other synthetic opioids include tramadol, which is used to treat moderate to severe pain; meperidine, which is sold under the brand name of Demerol; and fentanyl.

This was once a field of bright-red poppies. Now the fat seed pods will be harvested and sliced open so the milky sap (which is raw opium) can be removed.

Of all the opioids that exist, fentanyl is the most powerful—and because of that, it is also the most dangerous. Fentanyl was first introduced during the 1960s as an intravenous anesthetic to be used for patients who were undergoing surgery. It remained an important drug for medical use and for relieving the severe pain of patients for whom other types of opioids were not effective. Then, during the early years of the twenty-first century, there was an increase in reports of fentanyl being produced and sold illegally. From 2005 to 2007 the DEA linked more than one thousand deaths with illicitly produced fentanyl. From that point on, fentanyl-related deaths continued to increase year after year.

The National Institute on Drug Abuse (NIDA) says that fentanyl is relatively cheap to produce, which is why it is often mixed in with other street drugs. Another reason other drugs are cut with fentanyl is because it boosts their potency. The higher potency makes the drugs more addictive—and therefore increases demand by addicted users, which puts more money in the pockets of drug dealers. It is common for heroin to be laced with fentanyl, and fentanyl has been found in a number of other drugs as well. This is especially frightening because people taking the drugs are often unaware that the drugs have been cut with fentanyl. "With any given drug purchase, people don't know what they're getting," says Ciccarone. "It's sadly like 'Russian roulette.'"[7]

Fentanyl is mixed not only with opioids but also with many other types of drugs. In October 2018 eighteen people were treated for opioid overdose at a hospital emergency department in Philadelphia, Pennsylvania—and not one of them knew they had taken opioids. The patients had been smoking crack cocaine, which is not an opioid, and the drug had been laced with fentanyl. "None of them had intended to use opioids or fentanyl," says emergency medicine physician Utsha Khatri, "but their drug testing as well as their clinical presentation argued they had been exposed to pretty high doses of fentanyl."[8]

> "Whether it's cocaine, or you think it's heroin, or you think it's pills, it's gonna have fentanyl in it."[9]
>
> —Justin Herdman, a US attorney in Cleveland, Ohio

DEA officers have increasingly found fentanyl mixed in with drugs that are confiscated during major drug busts. According to the American Medical Association, 70 percent of cocaine-related deaths have involved fentanyl. In a 2018 bulletin, the DEA noted a 112 percent increase in the finding of cocaine and fentanyl together in drug samples. In April 2019 DEA officials in New Jersey confiscated 116 pounds (53 kg) of cocaine and fentanyl in a truckload of Tupperware containers. "Whether it's cocaine, or you think it's heroin, or you think it's pills, it's gonna have fentanyl in it,"[9] says Justin Herdman, a US attorney in Cleveland, Ohio.

How People Get Opioids

Those who need and/or want opioids can get them in different ways, depending on whether their intended use is legitimate or not. Medical or dental patients who suffer from pain can get a prescription for opioid painkillers from their doctor or dentist. They can use the prescription to get drugs from a local pharmacy or order them from a regulated online pharmacy. If pain sufferers visit an emergency room, a physician may prescribe opioids.

People who have become dependent on opioids sometimes continue to get them from their doctors. According to the Substance Abuse and Mental Health Services Administration, from 22 percent to 35 percent of opioid abusers continue to get a doctor's prescription for the drugs. Another 50 percent get opioids free from a friend or relative, and the rest either buy or steal the drugs from a friend or relative, buy them from a drug dealer or other stranger, or get them from more than one doctor.

People who seek to obtain illicit opioids often buy the drugs from dealers. According to the DEA, the biggest source for these opioids is Mexico, where numerous clandestine laboratories

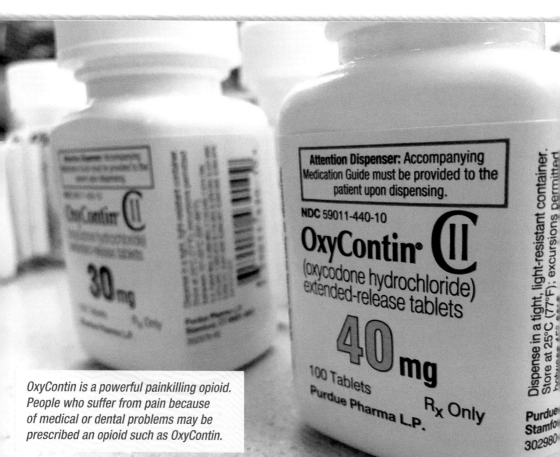

OxyContin is a powerful painkilling opioid. People who suffer from pain because of medical or dental problems may be prescribed an opioid such as OxyContin.

manufacture them. The drugs are then smuggled into the United States. The DEA reports that US border agents have been intercepting increasing amounts of fentanyl that traffickers have attempted to smuggle into the country, often in trucks carrying produce. In February 2018 the Mexican army seized a commercial truck and trailer that contained a shipment of avocados heading for the US border. The shipment was found to contain 1,977 pounds (897 kg) of cocaine, 89.5 pounds (40.6 kg) of fentanyl powder, 9.5 pounds (4.3 kg) of heroin, and approximately fifty-two hundred pills containing fentanyl. In January 2019 US border agents in Arizona seized 254 pounds (115 kg) of fentanyl powder and pills hidden in a truck that was loaded with cucumbers.

Illicit drug buyers also get opioids by ordering from unscrupulous online sellers, who often peddle drugs on a hidden part of the internet known as the Dark Web. Most of these drugs are made in laboratories in China and are shipped to the United States via the US Postal Service, FedEx, or commercial courier services.

Alarming Facts About Kids

As health officials and researchers monitor the opioid problem in the United States, they have made it a priority to closely watch opioid activity among young people. One study from May 2019, which focused on opioid prescriptions among teens and young adults, had some startling revelations. The researchers found that from 2005 to 2015, 57 million visits to doctors' offices and emergency rooms by teens and college students resulted in opioid prescriptions. This high prevalence is troubling to experts because the younger people are when they first start taking opioids, the greater their risk for becoming dependent on them. Deanna Wilson, a physician and addiction specialist in Pittsburgh, Pennsylvania, says that adolescents are especially vulnerable to addictive drugs because their brains have not finished developing. "Think of it as a car that has a gas pedal but the brakes aren't fully developed," says Wilson. She adds that another risk for young people who take opioids is their vulnerability to becoming addicted to heroin.

"The vast majority of young adult and adolescent patients using fentanyl and heroin started with a prescription for opioids,"[10] she says.

One piece of news about opioids that appears promising is that the rate of opioid abuse is starting to decline among high school students. For instance, the US Department of Health and Human Services reports that abuse of painkillers among high school seniors decreased from 9.5 percent in 2004 to 3.4 percent in 2018. High school seniors also reported that opioids were harder for them to get than in the past. In 2010, 54 percent of students in twelfth grade believed that these drugs were easily accessible, and by 2018 that number had dropped to 32.5 percent.

The Deadliest of the Deadly

Health officials and health care professionals are alarmed about the growing prevalence of fentanyl because of its strong potency and high potential to kill. Especially alarming is the proliferation of carfentanil, an extremely potent and lethal form of fentanyl. Carfentanil is used as a tranquilizer for elephants and other large animals and is at least one hundred times more powerful than fentanyl. It is such a dangerous substance that when veterinarians and other large animal professionals work with it, they must wear gear to protect their faces and bodies. This, says the executive director of the American Association of Zoo Veterinarians, is because "even one drop splattered into a person's eye or nose could be fatal."

In August 2016 border agents in Vancouver, Canada, seized a shipment of carfentanil that originated somewhere in China. In a package falsely marked "printer accessories," the shipment contained 2.2 pounds (1 kg) of carfentanil. This is equivalent to 50 million doses of the drug—which Canadian law enforcement officials say is enough to kill everyone in Canada.

Quoted in Rachel Browne, "Canada Just Seized 50 Million Doses of the Elephant Tranquilizer That's Killing People," Vice, August 9, 2016. www.vice.com.

As promising as this decline is, a revelation from a December 2018 study was alarming. Researchers from the Yale School of Medicine found that from 1999 to 2016 nearly nine thousand children and teens had died from overdoses of prescription painkillers and/or illicitly manufactured synthetic opioids—a 268 percent increase in seventeen years. Of the teens, most of the deaths were due to overdose of heroin or synthetic drugs such as fentanyl. The children were probably either given opioids by their parents or found opioid pills in their homes and swallowed them.

A Bleak Outlook

Research has clearly shown that people all over the United States have abused opioids. There are, however, some areas of the country that have been hit especially hard with opioid abuse, addiction, and overdose deaths. One of them is West Virginia, which has the tragic distinction of being the state with the highest number of overdose deaths related to opioids. According to a March 2019 publication by the NIDA, there were 833 drug overdose deaths involving opioids in West Virginia in 2017. That was a rate of 49.6 deaths per 100,000 people, and it was double the rate from 2019 and triple the national average of 14.6 deaths per 100,000 people. Other states where the opioid problem has reached crisis levels are Ohio and Kentucky, as well as New Hampshire, Maine, Massachusetts, Pennsylvania, Connecticut, and Rhode Island. "The level of death and despair in certain parts of the country is unfathomable,"[11] says Ciccarone.

"The level of death and despair in certain parts of the country is unfathomable."[11]

—Daniel Ciccarone, a physician and public health researcher from San Francisco

There is no doubt that the opioid abuse situation in the United States is an ongoing crisis. Although overall opioid use has decreased slightly, abuse of fentanyl is soaring. Whereas teen use of opioids has gone down, the number of opioid-related overdose deaths nearly tripled from 1999 to 2017. Clearly, the country is in the grip of an opioid abuse epidemic—and ending it will be no simple task.

CHAPTER TWO

Highly Addictive Drugs

Being addicted to drugs is a terrible, miserable condition. When someone is addicted, getting drugs becomes his or her sole reason for existing. Nothing else matters: not family, not friends, not employment or school or hobbies. Even using drugs stops being the pleasant experience it once was and instead becomes a driving physical need, something addicts feel they cannot survive without—even if they know it is killing them. "How do you know you're an addict? It's when . . . you're doing something that you know is not good for you, that's harming you, but you can't help yourself," says pain medicine specialist Deeni Bassam. "When your relationships are starting to fall apart around you, and you don't care. And the only thing that's on your mind is about how to get the substance and how to get to the next high— you're an addict."[12]

No Way to Live

Cortney Lovell knows firsthand the horrors of being an addict, and she now devotes time to warning others about it. Lovell got addicted to opioids when she was sixteen years old. Her girlfriend gave her a prescription painkiller tablet and assured her that it was perfectly safe because it was prescribed by a doctor. "But that pill flipped a switch inside me," says Lovell, "that took away my emotional pain and made me numb."[13]

Lovell had been abused as a child and says she had trauma that was largely unaddressed. Since the eighth grade she had suffered from a mood disorder, and she liked the feeling the pill gave her. She never even considered that it might be harmful or addictive. "I knew hard drugs were illegal and taboo, but I didn't think that *these* pills were dangerous," she says. "I had no idea that I could actually get addicted—I just knew that I felt sick when I stopped taking them." (Drug addicts use "sick" as a slang term for suffering from withdrawal.) Within three years, Lovell's drug addiction had taken over her life, and she lost interest in everything except getting high. "I went from being an honors student and varsity athlete, to a high school dropout in just one year," she says. "I tried to go to college after getting my GED, but my life revolved around using pills. I was so dependent on the pills that I became a shell of the person I used to be."[14]

> "My life revolved around using pills. I was so dependent on the pills that I became a shell of the person I used to be."[14]
>
> —Cortney Lovell, a recovering opioid addict from Albany, New York

Lovell's depiction of herself as a "shell of the person" she used to be is typical of many who become addicted to opioids. They reach a point that the only thing that matters is taking drugs. Addicts are often convinced that their very survival depends on taking opioids, and they are determined to keep taking them no matter the consequences. At her lowest point, Lovell was living with a gang, was running from twenty-seven felony charges, and had warrants for her arrest in four counties. By the time she took steps to turn her life around, she had stopped eating and lost weight, and her skin had turned redundant gray. "My eyes sank into the sockets, and my hair became so brittle," she says. "Even worse, my personality was not there anymore, I was only functioning to get money to get more opioids to prevent getting sick."[15]

21

The Addicted Brain

The reason for an addict's overpowering need for opioids is that the drugs cause brain chemistry to go haywire. For the brain to function normally, an intricate network of nerve cells, known as neurons, continuously send and receive messages in the form of electrical signals. This constant communication is made possible by chemicals known as neurotransmitters, which orchestrate the transfer of signals from one neuron to another. When neurotransmitters bind to proteins called receptors, they trigger changes in the cells. In reward regions of the brain, an excitatory cellular change takes place, meaning cells are activated—or excited. When someone gets a welcome surprise, is anticipating a fun event, or even enjoys a scrumptious dessert, it triggers an excitatory reaction in the brain. A neurotransmitter called dopamine binds to receptors, thereby sending dopamine molecules surging through the bloodstream. This results in feelings of exhilaration and an overall sense of happiness and well-being.

This normal brain activity is hijacked when someone takes opioids. The chemical structure of an opioid mimics that of natu-

When people who are addicted to drugs are suffering from withdrawal, they refer to it as being "sick."

ral neurotransmitters, and the similarity "tricks" receptors into allowing opioid molecules to bind to them. The brain floods the body with dopamine, which causes a heightened state of euphoria. Experts say that opioids can cause the release of up to ten times the dopamine that natural processes release, and it happens more quickly. Although this may produce an incredible high for the opioid user, the euphoria is short lived. Brain receptors become overwhelmed, and the brain's response is to produce less dopamine—or even eliminate dopamine receptors altogether.

As time goes by, the addict craves more opioids in a desperate attempt to feel the same euphoria as the first time. It is a futile effort, however, because euphoric feelings lessen as dopamine declines. The inevitable result is an addiction that grows so overpowering it completely consumes the person's life. "It was like the high put on blinders to everything and made me not care about anything in the world, other than the heroin,"[16] says Brandon N., a twenty-six-year-old opioid addict from Pennsylvania.

All opioids are highly addictive because of the way they interfere with brain function. But many drug experts consider fentanyl to be the most addictive of them all. Like other opioids, fentanyl binds to brain receptors, but it is far more powerful—about one hundred times stronger than morphine and fifty times stronger than heroin. The more potent an opioid, the greater the chance that users will become addicted to it. In fact, according to a former DEA officer, getting someone off heroin is easy compared to the arduous task of getting a person off fentanyl.

Brain Study Revelations

Because of how dangerous and addictive fentanyl and other opioids are, scientists are aggressively researching how they affect brain chemistry. One promising study was conducted in 2018 by researchers from the University of California, San Francisco (UCSF). The study revealed that neurons react differently to neurotransmitters than they do to opioid drugs: semisynthetic opioids such as morphine and heroin and purely synthetic opioids like fentanyl. These findings could help explain why people so easily get addicted to opioids.

The researchers, led by UCSF psychiatry professor Mark von Zastrow, wanted to find out whether all opioids (natural or synthetic) bind to the same receptors in neurons. To test this theory, they designed a tiny sensor called a nanobody that also binds to receptors. The sensor generated a fluorescent signal when an opioid receptor was activated. This allowed the researchers to look more closely than ever before at what happens on the surface of neurons, as well as inside them.

Using the nanobody, the researchers made a fascinating observation. They could see that synthetic opioid molecules activated receptors not just on the surface of cells but also inside of them. Also, synthetic opioids activated receptors in a different cellular location, where neurotransmitters produced no activation at all. These findings were astounding because they contradicted prevailing scientific beliefs about brain function. "There has been no evidence so far that opioid drugs do anything other than what natural opioids do," says von Zastrow, "so it's been hard to reconcile the experiences that drug users describe." He goes on to say that this study was intriguing because it confirmed what opioid users had been saying all along: that the effects of opioid drugs are "more intensely pleasurable than any naturally rewarding experience that they've ever had."[17]

The UCSF study is considered groundbreaking because of what it revealed about the effects of natural mood boosters versus synthetic opioids. Researchers hope that as they learn more about how opioids affect brain chemistry, it could lead to the development of safer, less addictive opioid medications, as well as better treatments for opioid addiction. "This is an area that hasn't been explored in drug development because people haven't been thinking about it," says von Zastrow, "but the potential is there."[18]

America's Long History with Opioid Addiction

The opioid epidemic that is in full swing in the United States is not the country's first struggle with such a crisis. That actually occurred during the Civil War, which lasted from 1861 to 1865. During the war, tens of thousands of soldiers were wounded and given opium or morphine on the battlefield and in field hospitals. Many returned home hopelessly addicted to opioids or became addicted later after being treated with morphine for war wounds. These wounds, which were either physical, psychological, or both, were often referred to as "soldier's disease."

One Union soldier who had been a prisoner of war for ten months became addicted to opium while he was hospitalized. After the war was over, he remained addicted and began using a hypodermic syringe to take the drug. His life was miserable, so he decided to give up opium by quitting cold turkey—and found the withdrawal to be horrific. In an 1876 book, he wrote, "No tongue or pen will ever describe . . . the depths of horror in which my life was plunged at this time; the days of humiliation and anguish, nights of terror and agony, through which I dragged my wretched being."

Anonymous, *Opium Eating: An Autobiographical Sketch.* Philadelphia: Claxton, Remsen, and Haffelfinger, 1876.

The Vulnerable Teen Brain

Although people of all ages can become addicted to opioids, young people are much more vulnerable than older adults. This is because their brains have not finished developing yet, which is a fact that scientists have only known since the 1990s. Before that, it was widely believed that the human brain was finished developing by the time a person reached puberty. Years of brain research revealed that to be untrue, and it is now known the brain is not fully developed until people are in their mid-twenties. "The teenage brain is really in a unique developmental stage that is still very much under construction,"[19] says Frances Jensen, a neurologist and expert on brain development. The part of the brain that is still undeveloped in teens is the part that enables them to make good decisions—including whether to take drugs or turn away from them.

The human brain develops from back to front. In the front section, areas known as the prefrontal and frontal cortexes are the last part to fully mature. This region of the brain controls reasoning, decision-making, and impulse control, whereas the back region controls emotion and motivation. So while the back of the brain may motivate a teen to throw caution to the wind and try

Teens who get hooked on opioids can have a really tough time coping. Researchers now know that young people have a higher risk of becoming addicted because their brains are not fully developed.

all kinds of new things, the front of the brain could urge the teen to think carefully and be cautious—if it were fully developed, which it is not.

Along with increasing young people's vulnerability to addiction, opioids can also harm their still-developing brains. According to NIDA director Nora Volkow, teen brains are susceptible to being "radically changed by drug use—often specifically by impeding the development of the very circuits that enable adults to say 'later' . . . or 'not at all' . . . to dangerous or unhealthy options." Consequently, says Volkow, when drug abuse begins at a young age, it can become a particularly "vicious cycle," as she explains: "Research shows that the earlier a teen first uses drugs, the likelier he or she is to become addicted to them or to become addicted to another substance later in life."[20]

Addiction Risk Factors

Along with young age, a number of other factors can increase people's vulnerability to becoming addicted to opioids. These may include genetic factors such as a family history of drug abuse; psychological factors such as a history of severe depression, anxiety, or substance abuse; personality traits like risk-taking or thrill-seeking behavior; and environmental factors such as stressful life circumstances, poverty, unemployment, or regular contact with people who abuse drugs.

Addiction experts say that women have a higher risk of becoming addicted to opioids than men. One reason for this is that women are more likely to suffer from chronic pain and seek opioids for pain relief. As a result, they are more likely than men to be prescribed opioid painkillers, to be given the drugs for longer periods of time, and to be given higher doses. "Women may also have biological tendencies to become dependent on prescription pain relievers more quickly than men,"[21] says the Mayo Clinic.

The Growing Incidence of Drug Diversion

Another strong risk factor for addiction is someone's work environment. Research has shown, for instance, that health care professionals have a markedly higher risk of becoming addicted to opioids compared with those who do not work in the health care industry. A May 2019 report by the data firm Protenus showed that drug diversion, which refers to a health care worker's stealing drugs from the hospital's supply, is a serious and growing problem in health care. Protenus found that in 2018 more than 47 million doses of opioids were stolen—an increase of 126 percent over the year before. Another finding was that more than one-third of these incidents happened at hospitals or medical centers. The remaining drug thefts took place at private medical practices, long-term care facilities, and pharmacies. The most common drugs illegally taken were oxycodone, hydrocodone, and fentanyl (in that order). In nearly 70 percent of the cases, doctors and nurses committed the thefts.

Research has shown that millions of doses of prescription opioids are diverted (stolen) from hospitals, pharmacies, and medical centers each year. In the majority of cases, doctors or nurses committed the thefts.

A Tragic Story of Opioid Addiction

Nichole Lynn Halter, or Nikki, as she was known, died at age twenty-six from a fentanyl overdose. To those who knew her, Nikki was not at all someone they would suspect of being an addict. She was a critical care nurse at a major health care system in Indianapolis, Indiana. She was studying to complete her bachelor's degree in nursing. And she was a loving, devoted mother to her six-year-old son, Colton. "Nikki was the picture of success," says her mother, Janet Edwards. "But even with a thriving personal and professional life, she kept a secret that would eventually take her life—an addiction to opioids."

Feeling overwhelmed by her impossibly crammed schedule, Nikki saw a doctor and obtained prescriptions for two nonopioid drugs, Xanax and Adderall. She became addicted to both and found a way to get prescriptions from multiple physicians. Over time, Nikki's addiction escalated to fentanyl, which she had begun to steal from the hospital where she worked. In June 2014 she died of a fentanyl overdose. "Like many others, Nikki didn't show any signs of addiction—not at home nor in the workplace," says Edwards, who is now painfully aware that signs of addiction may be carefully hidden—sometimes with tragic results.

Janet Edwards, "Saving a Life from Opioid Addiction Requires a Bold Action from Loved Ones," *Health Affairs*, September 9, 2019. www.healthaffairs.org.

One such doctor was Stephen Loyd from eastern Tennessee. Because of a high-stress job, long working hours, and efforts to juggle work and family life, he was burned out. On one particularly stressful day, Loyd took one-half of a hydrocodone pain pill that his dentist had given him several weeks before. He still remembers an immediate sense of relief—and he now knows that was the beginning of his opioid addiction. "What I didn't realize was how quickly it would escalate,"[22] he says.

When his bottle of hydrocodone pills was gone, Loyd started taking prescription pills from his aunt's medicine cabinet. Then he began taking pills from the medical office where he worked. For the next three and a half years, he continued taking pills from work. By the time his father finally confronted him about his drug problem, Loyd was taking about 500 milligrams of OxyContin per day. "That's about 100 Vicodin," he says. Sometimes he swallowed a handful of pills at once, and other times he crushed them and snorted them. He was able to get clean with professional help and says his experience as an addict has given him empathy for others who are slaves to addiction. "I know what it's like to want to stop and can't," says Loyd. "I know what it's like to want to die. I know the shame and guilt."[23]

An Agonizing Struggle

Although every person who gets addicted to opioids has his or her own unique story, what Loyd describes is typical. No one starts out expecting to become an addict—and no one would voluntarily choose to be an addict. Once addiction has taken hold, few people can easily walk away from it. Opioid addiction changes the chemistry of the brain and in the process makes the user feel like nothing else matters but getting high.

CHAPTER THREE

The High Risks of Opioid Abuse

With opioid-related overdose deaths at an all-time high, health officials continue to watch this epidemic closely. New data about the prevalence of opioid abuse and/or drug overdose deaths involving opioids is publicized in reports. But one particular kind of information on opioids is not tracked and is therefore largely unknown to the public: the number of people who suffer from severe health problems because of opioid abuse or opioid overdoses in which the person survived. Contrary to what many people believe, overdose does not always result in death—but people who survive are often left with permanent health damage. "We focus on deaths but we forget that there's another group of people who have been negatively impacted, some of them severely,"[24] says Patricia Daly, chief medical health officer of a health care system in Vancouver, Canada.

> "We focus on deaths but we forget that there's another group of people who have been negatively impacted, some of them severely."[24]
>
> —Patricia Daly, the chief medical health officer of a health care system in Vancouver, Canada

Plenty of Anecdotal Evidence

Even in the absence of hard data on opioid-related health problems, Daly, her colleagues, and other health care practitioners are well aware of what opioid abuse can do

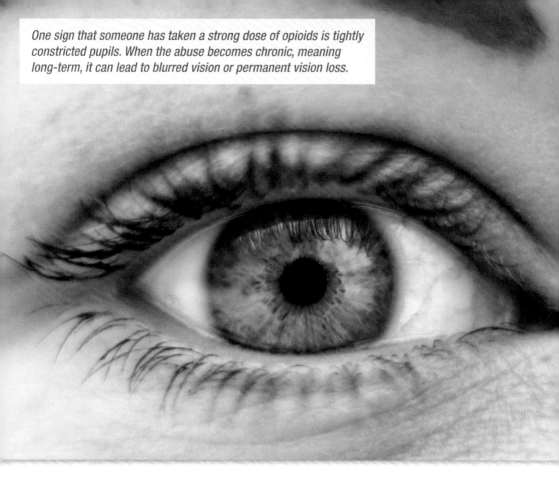

One sign that someone has taken a strong dose of opioids is tightly constricted pupils. When the abuse becomes chronic, meaning long-term, it can lead to blurred vision or permanent vision loss.

to people's health. Whether they work in emergency rooms, physician offices, clinics, or other health care facilities, they see the devastating harm of opioid abuse on a daily basis.

Opioid abuse is associated with numerous health issues, many of which are life threatening. People who abuse these drugs may suffer from cardiovascular problems such as irregular heartbeat, which can increase their risk for heart attack. Opioid abuse may result in damage to the digestive system, kidneys, liver, and blood. The tightly constricted pupils that are characteristic of opioid abuse can lead to blurred vision or even permanent vision loss. Opioids also interfere with the ability to breathe normally, which impairs normal lung function and can lead to pneumonia. Another very real risk of opioid abuse—and one of the most devastating—is permanent, irreversible brain damage.

Lives Forever Changed

Whenever someone abuses opioids, the greatest risk is that they will overdose, which happens when a dangerously high amount of a drug enters a person's system. An overdose causes breathing to abnormally slow, which in turn reduces oxygen levels in the bloodstream. If the person is not revived quickly, oxygen starvation can damage vital organs like the kidneys, liver, and heart. These organs begin shutting down in order to preserve oxygen for brain tissue. If too much time passes and the person does not start breathing normally, this can result in a condition known as hypoxia, in which too little oxygen reaches the brain.

In order to function, brain cells need a constant supply of oxygen, so they are extremely sensitive to its depletion. Without enough oxygen, brain cells die quickly; sometimes within thirty seconds of losing their oxygen supply. "Hypoxia can have short- and long-term psychological and neurological effects," says NIDA, "including coma, permanent brain damage, or death."[25] Patients who are revived after an overdose may suffer from health problems that range from memory loss and hand tremors to a permanent vegetative state.

The latter describes many patients taken care of by Caroline O. McCagg, associate medical director at JFK Medical Center in Edison, New Jersey. McCagg oversees patients with brain trauma, including those whose trauma was caused by a drug overdose. Some of these patients do get better, she says, but they are so cognitively impaired that their communication is limited and they are unlikely to be able to live independently. McCagg does not mince words when explaining how much these patients' lives have deteriorated—"a living death" is how she describes their condition. "They don't always come back all the way," she says. "I've had patients for 10 or 15 years

> "Hypoxia can have short- and long-term psychological and neurological effects, including coma, permanent brain damage, or death."[25]
>
> —National Institute on Drug Abuse, the United States' leading research organization on drug abuse and addiction

who are just in limbo. But the family can't let them go. Death would be kind, in some instances."[26]

Amanda Wright sustained permanent brain damage after an opioid overdose, but the damage was not as severe as that of many of McCagg's patients. Wright became addicted to oxycodone as a teenager when she was badly injured in a car accident. When her prescription ran out, she started buying the drug on the street, and later she switched to fentanyl. In September 2017, when Wright was twenty-nine, she snorted a near-fatal dose of fentanyl. She happened to be at her parents' home when this occurred, and her father found her crumpled and unresponsive on the kitchen floor.

Wright's mother, Liana Wright, is a coroner and former emergency room nurse, so she knew her daughter had overdosed when she saw her purple face, pinpoint pupils, and lack of pulse. Liana was able to revive Amanda but says about ten minutes passed before she started breathing. The lack of oxygen caused such severe brain damage that Amanda could not remember how to take a shower, brush her teeth, or answer very basic questions. She improved significantly after months of rehabilitation but has permanent brain damage. Thus, she will forever have to live with the effects of her overdose and will probably never be able to hold a full-time job or live independently.

The Dangers of Shooting Up

As with Amanda Wright, many people who become addicted to opioids start with prescription painkillers. When they can no longer get the drugs legally, they turn to illicit opioids—often heroin because it is much cheaper to buy on the street than counterfeit painkillers. The health risks associated with heroin are numerous, and people who inject it have the highest risk of all. Injecting heroin into a vein, which is often called shooting up, increases the risk of exposure to HIV, the virus that causes AIDS; viral hepatitis, an infectious disease of the liver; and other types of infections. Shooting heroin can lead to collapsed veins and a condition known as venous sclerosis, which results in narrowing and hardening of the

Musician Deaths from Fentanyl

As tragic as it is when beloved musicians die from an overdose, it is not a new phenomenon. Whether it involved alcohol, heroin, cocaine, or other drugs, celebrity overdose deaths have occurred for as long as there were celebrities. But from 2016 to 2018, a shocking number of famous musicians died from an overdose that involved fentanyl. This was true of the superstar musician Prince. For years he aggressively jumped around onstage during live performances, and his body took a beating, so he started taking prescription painkillers. When he died in April 2016, it was from an overdose of counterfeit Vicodin laced with fentanyl. The following year, in October 2017, musician Tom Petty died in a nearly identical way: overdose of a painkiller laced with fentanyl.

In November 2017 rising rapper Lil Peep was found dead on his tour bus. His death was later determined to be from a lethal combination of fentanyl and the antianxiety drug Xanax. The chart-topping rapper Mac Miller died in September 2018. Toxicology reports later showed that his death was caused by a combination of fentanyl, cocaine, and alcohol. Pop culture writer Rae Alexandra opines, "As long as fentanyl keeps showing up in drugs that are supposed to be significantly less potent, the list of stars lost too soon is bound to get longer."

Rae Alexandra, "Celebrity Fentanyl Use Isn't Rooted in Hedonism. It's Desperation," KQED Arts, February 6, 2019. www.kqed.org.

veins. Permanent scarring from repeated injections is also a common effect of shooting heroin.

One of the deadliest risks of injecting heroin is endocarditis, which is a severe bacterial infection of the heart valves. Once relatively rare, the infection is becoming more common among people who inject drugs. According to a September 2019 report in the *Journal of the American Heart Association*, the prevalence of drug abuse–related endocarditis nearly doubled from 2002 to 2016. One of the people who contracted it is Jerika Whitefield, a

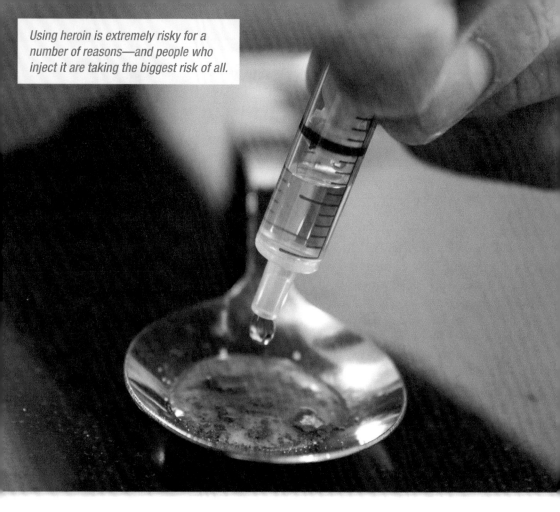

woman from Oak Ridge, Tennessee, who has battled opioid addiction since she was a teenager. In June 2016 Whitefield developed endocarditis after a drug injection, but doctors saved her life. She stayed clean but two months later was showing signs of heart failure. A doctor performed open-heart surgery, and although he was compassionate, he emphasized that he would only operate on Whitefield once. If she went back to shooting up, he would not perform surgery again.

Maimed by Opioid Abuse

Some of the most crippling effects of opioid abuse are virtually unknown to the general public. People who are well aware of the risks of sharing needles and the dangers of overdose have likely never heard of something called rhabdo, which is short for rhabdomyolysis, a syndrome that is caused by injuries to skeletal muscles. It is a risk for people who abuse opioids because if they overdose and crumple to the ground, they may lie immobile for a long time before someone finds them. Often when this happens the person who overdosed is positioned in such a way that circulation is cut off to his or her limbs. This can lead to rhabdo—and sometimes permanent crippling injuries.

This is what happened to Lisa, a woman from Somerville, Massachusetts, who overdosed on opioids in 2013. Her daughter found her slumped over the washing machine and took her to bed without realizing that one leg was bent under Lisa's body. She lay like that, in the same position, for more than a day. When her daughter checked to make sure Lisa was still breathing, she noticed that the leg looked white and shriveled. She began massaging it vigorously, which probably saved it from having to be amputated. "If she hadn't done that, I don't think I'd be walking on this leg," says Lisa. "I think I would have killed it."[27] She now walks with a limp because of permanent damage to her muscles and nerves.

Jared, who also overdosed on opioids and also sustained muscle damage from rhabdo, suffered much more debilitating injuries than Lisa did. In April 2016 he overdosed on a potent mixture of heroin and prescription opioids. He remembers sitting down on a stairway to smoke a cigarette, and his memory is blank after that. When someone found him, he was bent in half, with his upper body in between his legs—which had cut off circulation to the lower half of his body for up to eight hours. At the hospital, Jared remained in a coma and on life support for weeks. Because so much time had passed without circulation in his lower body, both of his legs had to be amputated.

Damage to Kidneys and Liver

Another life-threatening condition that can develop with the onset of rhabdo is kidney failure. Whenever circulation is cut off for a long period of time, the resulting breakdown of muscle tissue releases chemicals into the bloodstream. "They can clog up the filtration system in the kidneys," says Melisa Lai-Becker, emergency department chief at Cambridge Health Alliance in Everett, Massachusetts. "And when that happens, the kidneys can shut down completely."[28] The main function of the kidneys is to help filter toxins and waste from the body. When the kidneys are not working properly, it can be life threatening.

Another major organ that acts as a filter is the liver—and it, too, can be damaged by opioid abuse. The liver has hundreds of functions, such as filtering blood coming from the digestive tract before passing it to the rest of the body. Anything that people consume, whether it is food, alcohol, drugs, or toxins, is digested by the stomach and small intestine, absorbed into the blood, and then transported to the liver. Some substances that end up in the liver can be especially damaging to it, such as opioids that contain acetaminophen. Research has shown that people who abuse Vicodin, which is a combination of acetaminophen and hydrocodone, are at risk of developing liver disease. And because alcohol is also toxic to the liver, those who use acetaminophen-containing opioids and drink alcohol have an even higher risk.

Perilous Unknowns

Of all the dangerous risks involved with taking illicit opioids, not having the slightest idea how they were made or what is in them is among the worst. Most of these drugs are made in China, where there is no government control over content, quality, or sanitation in manufacturing plants. So when people order illicit opioids from online sellers or buy them from a dealer, they are putting substances in their bodies that could contain everything from powdered milk or talcum powder to amounts of fentanyl that could cause instant death.

Too many deaths from opioid overdose is what motivated Matt Cronin to investigate where the drugs were coming from. Cronin is an assistant US attorney and national opioid coor-

Accidental Overdose or Suicide?

In a September 2019 paper, two of the United States' leading health officials discussed the likelihood that a high number of opioid overdose deaths could have been suicides. Coauthors Joshua Gordon, director of the National Institute of Mental Health, and Nora Volkow, director of the National Institute of Drug Abuse, emphasized that the opioid overdose epidemic is not limited to people who accidentally take too much of a prescription opioid or inject too much heroin. According to Gordon and Volkow, experts estimate that up to 30 percent of opioid overdoses could be suicides.

Mady Ohlman, a young woman from Massachusetts, says that many drug abusers reach a point that their addiction and continuous pursuit of illegal drugs wears on them until it crushes their will to live. She was twenty-two when, after being addicted to opioids for more than three years, she decided to give up on life. She got needles ready with heroin and planned to intentionally overdose. She has no memory of how much heroin she injected before collapsing, nor does she know how long she lay unconscious on the floor. But she does remember wanting to die. "You realize getting clean would be a lot of work," says Ohlman. "And you realize dying would be a lot less painful. And you also feel like you'll be doing everyone else a favor if you die." To this day, she has no idea why the multiple injections did not kill her. "I just got really lucky," she says. "I don't know how."

Quoted in Martha Bebinger, "How Many Opioid Overdoses Are Suicides?," Kaiser Health News, March 28, 2018. https://khn.org.

dinator from Cleveland, Ohio. He made contact with a dealer who bragged about being able to get any kind of drug Cronin wanted from sellers in China. Cronin's investigators went online and sent a message per the dealer's instructions saying they wanted to buy fentanyl. Immediately, they received at least fifty replies from China-based drug traffickers, all saying they had all the fentanyl the buyers could want. One of the traffickers said he could provide any drug imaginable, including those that exist and those that do not exist. "He called it custom synthesis," says Cronin. "What it really meant was made-to-order poison."[29] It is doubtful that people who buy and use opioids realize they are taking poison. But by using substances they buy from a dealer or order online, they are risking their health and their lives.

The Ultimate Risk

For anyone who abuses opioids, the potential of dying from an overdose is extraordinarily high—even for those who only take the drugs one time. Although there is no way to know exactly

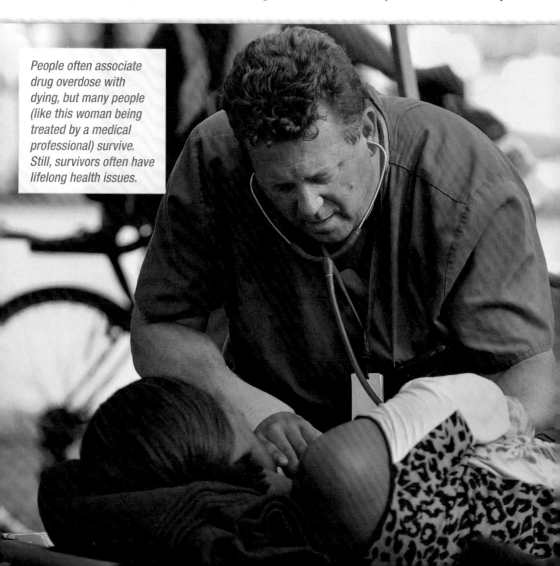

People often associate drug overdose with dying, but many people (like this woman being treated by a medical professional) survive. Still, survivors often have lifelong health issues.

how many opioid abusers overdose and survive, one statistic that health officials do know is this: every day of the year, more than 130 people in the United States die from overdosing on opioids. One of them was twenty-one-year-old Matt Ward, who died in May 2019 of fentanyl poisoning. Like so many opioid addicts, Ward had gotten hooked on prescription painkillers when he was in high school and had a tooth pulled. That escalated into an addiction and his death from an overdose. His distraught family is convinced that he had no idea there was fentanyl in the opioid that killed him.

Although not everyone who overdoses dies, people who abuse opioids are flirting with death every time they use. They also face innumerable health risks, including brain damage from hypoxia, kidney failure, exposure to HIV and hepatitis, and possible limb amputation from cut-off circulation after overdose. With the opioid epidemic still going strong, serious health issues are likely to get worse in the near future, rather than improve. "Unfortunately, this epidemic isn't going away any time soon," says physician and public health researcher Daniel Ciccarone, who has studied drug abuse for eighteen years. "That's one of the saddest insights I have."[30]

"Unfortunately, this epidemic isn't going away any time soon. That's one of the saddest insights I have."[30]

—Daniel Ciccarone, a physician and public health researcher

CHAPTER FOUR

Treatment and Recovery Challenges

As prevalent as opioid abuse has become in recent years, and with the dramatic rise in related overdose deaths, there is a vast and growing need for treatment. Yet only about one in ten people who need treatment for opioid addiction actually ever get it. To put that statistic in perspective, NIDA reports that more than 2 million people in the United States suffer from opioid use disorder (OUD). Only one out of ten receiving treatment means that 1.8 million others are not treated at all. In a September 2017 article on the STAT news website, psychiatrists Richard Ries and Andrew J. Saxon write, "Proper treatment for opioid addiction substantially reduces overdoses and can markedly improve lives, and even save them. Yet most individuals with this brain disease aren't getting any kind of treatment."[31]

Stigma and Other Frustrating Barriers

That such a vast number of people are not being treated for their opioid abuse or addiction is a complicated problem with many factors. One major reason why many people never seek treatment is the widespread stigma surrounding drug addiction. Stigma is defined as negative and often unfair beliefs about something or someone, like people who get addicted to drugs. These beliefs are stereotypical, judgmental, and often wrong. Assuming that everyone who is addicted to drugs chooses to live that way is an example of stigma; another is assuming that only lower-class people abuse drugs. Those who are caught in the grip of addiction are well aware of the stigma, and because of that, they are often too ashamed and embarrassed to ask anyone for help.

The stigma associated with drug addiction is often perpetuated by physicians and other health care providers. Among people suffering from OUD who have a regular physician (and many do not), it is not uncommon to encounter negative attitudes when broaching the subject of opioid abuse or addiction. If health care professionals do not respond with understanding and compassion, this feeds into the patient's shame and makes it even less likely he or she will reach out for help. "Medical providers often exhibit stigma related to patients with opioid addiction, too, making it difficult for patients to trust the treatment community," says Payel Roy, a physician and addiction medicine expert with Boston University School of Medicine. Roy sees patients every day who are struggling with OUD, and one of his greatest frustrations is the number of people who go without treatment when it could make such a difference in their lives. "Stigma gets in the way,"[32] he says.

"Medical providers often exhibit stigma related to patients with opioid addiction."[32]

—Payel Roy, a physician and addiction medicine expert with Boston University School of Medicine

Another challenge is that most physicians are not qualified to diagnose and/or treat patients who abuse and/or are addicted to drugs. Unless they are specialists, they are not trained in addiction medicine. Thus, the majority of doctors are not sure how to help patients or even where to refer them.

There are, of course, physicians who specialize in addiction medicine, but in the United States these specialists are rare. One of these rarities is Bradley M. Buchheit, a physician from Portland, Oregon. He made a conscious choice to focus on addiction

When people talk to their doctors about an opioid problem, they hope for understanding and compassion. It is not uncommon, however, for them to encounter negative attitudes because of the stigma associated with drug abuse and addiction.

medicine and finds the work gratifying and fulfilling. "I really enjoy working with these patients," says Buchheit. "They have often been kicked to the curb by the formal medical system. They don't trust us. So for them to walk into a room and have a doctor say, 'It's great to see you, thank you for coming in,' is very powerful. And then you can see them get better with treatment. It can be very rewarding work."[33]

A Confusing Maze of Choices

People suffering from OUD, along with their families, can become frustrated and overwhelmed at the process of finding help. The dearth of qualified addiction specialists is a problem, and even doctors who make referrals for addiction treatment programs are in extremely short supply. And there is no reliable, credible guide or directory that people can use to find treatment programs—or to weed out the good ones from those that are ineffective and even harmful.

According to a 2018 article by Sarah Wakeman, a physician and opioid addiction expert, and Gary Mendell, the chief executive officer of a nonprofit called Shatterproof, the people who get into treatment programs, and their families, often choose these programs without having any solid evidence about their effectiveness—even whether they have helped anyone. As the article states, "At a loss for real answers, thousands of Americans are forced to navigate a scattered system of 14,000 programs that aren't required to meet a standard set of medical qualifications."[34]

Kim and Tim Blake faced the daunting, frustrating task of hunting for rehabilitation facilities to help their son, Sean, who was addicted to heroin. The Blakes, who are from South Burlington, Vermont, had no idea where to start when they first began searching for treatment programs. Tim refers to that as "the beginning of this period of cycling through rehab after rehab after rehab."[35] They started with the one facility they had heard good things about, the Hazelden Betty Ford youth program in Minnesota. Sean was accepted by the facility but was accused of fighting and was kicked out after five weeks. The cost to the Blakes, even though Sean did not benefit from the program, was $36,000. Sean then went to a facility in Long Beach, California, called New Found Life. He seemed to be making progress there—but within a few months of being discharged, he was homeless and back to using drugs again. In neither of these situations did representatives from the treatment facilities follow up with Sean to see how he was doing.

"At a loss for real answers, thousands of Americans are forced to navigate a scattered system of 14,000 programs that aren't required to meet a standard set of medical qualifications."[34]

—Sarah Wakeman, a physician and opioid addiction expert, and Gary Mendell, the chief executive officer of the nonprofit Shatterproof

This exhausting, frustrating ordeal repeated itself over the next ten years. In that time Sean's parents sent him to more than a

The Horrors of Withdrawal

One of the most daunting hurdles for people trying to recover from opioid addiction is the prospect of going through withdrawal. Often referring to withdrawal as "dope sick," those who have endured it describe it in various ways, from getting a stomach flu on steroids to feeling so miserable they want to die. Although effects of withdrawal differ from person to person, some of the most common effects include vomiting, painful muscle aches, sweating alternating with chills, diarrhea, a runny nose, uncontrollable tremors, and severe anxiety. In some cases withdrawal can last for months, which makes it even more difficult to bear.

Allyson, a woman who started using heroin in her late teens, is a heroin addict who has gone through withdrawal more than once. She knows about the risk of using fentanyl and tries to stay away from it but says she will take most any drug to avoid the sheer misery of withdrawal. "It literally feels like your skin is crawling off," she says. "You're sweating profusely. Your nose is running, your eyes are running. And that's all you can focus on. You can't think."

Quoted in Martha Bebinger, "Another Circle of Hell: Surviving Opioids in the Fentanyl Era," Kaiser Health News, April 7, 2017. https://khn.org.

dozen rehabilitation facilities in five different states. As much as Sean wanted to recover, though, none of the programs worked for him, and eventually he lost his battle with opioid addiction. In August 2017, at age twenty-seven, Sean died of an overdose of alcohol combined with fentanyl.

During the decade that Sean was in the various drug rehabilitation facilities, his parents drained their savings. In addition to the $36,000 cost for the Hazelden Betty Ford youth program, they spent $20,000 on a wilderness program in Pennsylvania and more than $52,000 on New Found Life. They spent thousands of dollars more on other inpatient and outpatient treatment programs. Although their insurance covered some of the costs, the Blakes spent about $110,000 on futilely trying to help Sean get well. This is, unfortunately, typical of many who are desperately trying to get help for their loved ones. According to a 2019 investigation by the news site Vox, families throughout the United States are spending tens of thousands of dollars on addiction treatment that makes little to no difference. "In story after story," says Vox senior correspondent German Lopez, "the same experience was repeated over and over: of patients and families getting sucked into an American rehab industry that is largely unregulated, shockingly ineffective, and ruinously expensive."[36]

The Gold Standard

Many drug rehabilitation programs (like those where Sean Blake stayed) claim that they have helped many people recover from drug addiction, including addiction to opioids. The philosophy of these programs, including Hazelden Betty Ford, is typically based on a set of guiding principles known as the twelve steps. This treatment approach was originally developed by Alcoholics Anonymous as a recovery method for people whose lives were consumed by alcoholism. Although many people say they have benefited from the twelve-step approach when giving up alcohol, there is no evidence that the same approach works for people who are addicted to drugs. In fact, there is only one evidence-based approach to treating opioid use disorder: medication-assisted treatment, or MAT.

MAT is an approach to treating OUD that involves addiction counseling along with prescription medications. Because it has a high record of success, addiction experts and health officials often refer to MAT as the gold standard of OUD treatment, and they overwhelmingly support the approach. One avid MAT supporter is NIDA director Nora Volkow, who writes, "Medications cannot take the place of an individual's willpower, but they aid addicted individuals in resisting the constant challenges to their resolve. [The medications] have been shown in study after study to reduce illicit drug use and its consequences. They save lives."[37]

"Medications cannot take the place of an individual's willpower, but they aid addicted individuals in resisting the constant challenges to their resolve."[37]

—Nora Volkow, director of NIDA

Opioid addiction is extremely difficult to treat. People who receive treatment may get better— or end up homeless and back on the streets.

The US Food and Drug Administration has approved three medications for the treatment of opioid use disorder: methadone, buprenorphine, and naltrexone. Addiction specialists choose which medication to prescribe on the basis of a patient's level of addiction and his or her individual needs. "Just like if someone was sick with cancer, the treatment for that cancer would be based on how severe the cancer is," says Paula Cook, an addiction specialist with University of Utah Health. "With opioid addiction, we look at different factors, take all those things into consideration, and then make a recommendation."[38]

Methadone and buprenorphine are opioids, but they do not affect the body in the same way as other opioids. The brain responds differently to them than it does to other opioids such as heroin and fentanyl. Methadone and buprenorphine activate the same receptors as neurotransmitters (and opioid drugs) but are absorbed into the blood over a longer period of time. This helps prevent withdrawal symptoms and also breaks the psychological link between using a drug and immediately feeling high from it. "This allows the addicted brain to slowly begin to recover from all the highs and lows of opioid use so people are in a more 'normal,' steady state,"[39] says Payel Roy. Both methadone and buprenorphine are available by prescription. But under federal law, methadone may only be distributed by clinics that are certified by the Substance Abuse and Mental Health Services Administration.

Unlike methadone and buprenorphine, naltrexone is not an opioid. It is a narcotic blocker, or a drug that is known as an opioid antagonist. Naltrexone binds to brain receptors and sits on them; but rather than activating these receptors, it blocks them from being activated. So if a patient relapses and uses opioids, he or she will not feel anything—no euphoria or any other effects

The Debate over Addiction Treatment for Prisoners

Research has shown that at least one-fourth of the people who are incarcerated in the United States are addicted to heroin or other opioids. Yet according to the public policy organization Pew Charitable Trusts, fewer than 1 percent of the country's prisons and jails allow prisoners access to MAT with the drugs methadone and buprenorphine. Although these drugs are narcotics, they do not work the same way as addictive opioids and have been proved effective at helping people recover from opioid addiction.

An April 2018 Pew news story explains that standing in the way of MAT for addicted prisoners are sheriffs and other prison officials who have various reasons for their objections. One of them is James Cummings, a sheriff in Barnstable County, Massachusetts, who explains why he objects to MAT for prisoners: "We ruled out buprenorphine because it doesn't work for the people we deal with. Inmates try to smuggle it into the facility every day. It's a narcotic. They use it until they can get their next heroin fix so they don't get sick and they sell it to get money to buy more heroin. It's not a good fit."

Quoted in Christine Vestral, "New Momentum for Addiction Treatment Behind Bars," *Stateline* (blog), Pew Charitable Trusts, April 4, 2018. www.pewtrusts.org.

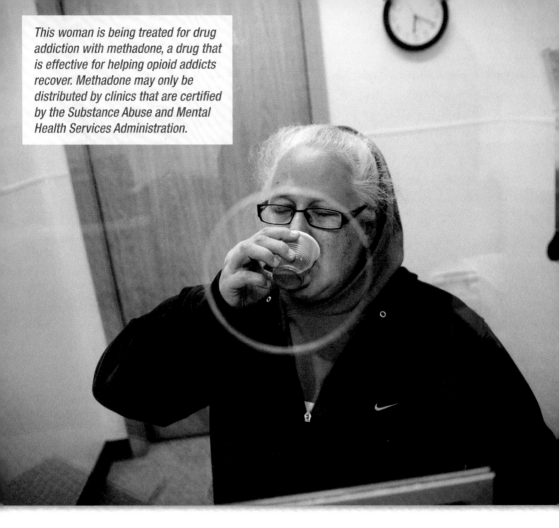

of getting high. In other words, naltrexone takes away the reward of getting high, which in turn will reduce the person's desire for the drug.

The Detractors

As strong and widespread as support is for the MAT approach to addiction treatment, not everyone favors it—in fact, objectors outnumber supporters. Counselors and rehabilitation facilities that espouse the twelve-step approach believe that those who take medication for addiction are not really sober; rather, they have just exchanged one addiction for another. "I could go on and on about this," says Roy. "When it comes to patients, there is still a lot of stigma around medications used to treat opioid use disorder. People feel that they are 'still addicted' if they use opioid-based medications like buprenorphine as treatment."[40]

Along with rehabilitation facilities, many doctors are also hesitant about treating OUD patients with medications. One of the biggest reasons for this is navigating the maze of government regulations. The restriction on methadone is one hurdle they have to clear, but it is not the only one. Physicians who want to prescribe buprenorphine must take an all-day training course and then obtain a special waiver from the DEA. According to pediatrician and addiction specialist Scott E. Hadland, taking these steps is rare among medical professionals. "Very few physicians in the United States have undergone this training," says Hadland, "and as a result, there are very few people eligible to prescribe these medications."[41]

MAT: Proven to Help Teens

There is even more resistance to using the MAT approach on young people who are addicted to opioids, as well as many more barriers to treatment. Also, according to Hadland, there is a stigma around prescribing these drugs for young people. He says doctors are often uncomfortable with this approach and/or feel that other non-drug approaches should be tried before resorting to medications.

Yet research has shown that the MAT approach can help teens with OUD where other treatment methods do not. A 2019 study by Hadland and his colleagues from Boston Medical Center in Massachusetts found that youth who received buprenorphine, naltrexone, or methadone were 42 percent, 46 percent, and 68 percent, respectively, more likely to stick with treatment, compared with those who were only treated with psychotherapy. Hadland says, "Our study demonstrates that, by providing medication as early as possible, youth are more strongly retained in treatment vs. behavioral treatment alone."[42] Just as he

"Our study demonstrates that, by providing medication as early as possible, youth are more strongly retained in treatment vs. behavioral treatment alone."[42]

—Scott E. Hadland, a pediatrician and addiction specialist

strongly favors the MAT approach for adults who are addicted to opioids, Hadland is convinced that it should be offered to youth suffering from OUD. But another finding of his study was that only one in four young adults and only one in twenty-one teens were offered medications for treatment.

Hope Dimmed by Reality

People who are addicted to opioids and/or are diagnosed with OUD can be effectively treated and can recover. Sadly, however, most never receive the treatment that could benefit them and possibly even save their lives. There are thousands of rehabilitation facilities but no way for people to find out whether the programs they offer are effective. Thus, people can—and do—spend thousands of dollars for programs that fail to help at all. The evidence is strong for medication-assisted treatment as an effective approach, but it still has many detractors, including health care providers. With the number of opioid-related overdose deaths close to fifty thousand, more reliable solutions to this crisis are desperately needed.

CHAPTER FIVE

The Fight to Prevent Opioid Abuse

As with all substance abuse, preventing opioid abuse before it starts is the best way to protect people from the dangers associated with the drugs. This is especially important for children and teenagers. Because their brains are not fully developed, they are especially vulnerable to addiction—and research has shown that about 90 percent of addictions start during the teenage years.

NIDA director Nora Volkow has written extensively about the opioid crisis in the United States and is fiercely devoted to finding ways to curtail the problem. In a June 2019 blog post, she discusses the importance of focusing on prevention. "As our communities, healthcare systems, and government agencies join in the effort to reverse the epidemic of opioid overdoses and solve the opioid crisis," says Volkow, "it is not enough to focus all our resources on treating people who are already addicted to opioids. Keeping people who do not have an opioid use disorder from becoming addicted is an equally important task." In the fight against opioid abuse, Volkow acknowledges the importance of addressing the overprescribing of pain medications and of reducing the supply of illicit opioids like heroin and fentanyl through law enforcement efforts. But, she adds, "reducing the demand for opioids by addressing the reasons people turn to them and become addicted in the first place is just as vital and fundamental to ensuring that a new drug epidemic does not follow once the opioid crisis is contained."[43]

Using Tragedy for Good

When someone has experienced an unthinkable tragedy such as losing a loved one to an opioid overdose, coping with the grief can seem impossible. Some people work through their grief by volunteering; they help prevent other families from going through the same terrible ordeal. This is true of Becky Savage of Granger, Indiana, who knows firsthand about this sort of unspeakable grief. In June 2015 Savage's nineteen-year-old son, Nick, died from accidentally overdosing on oxycodone at a party—and the same night, after the same party, she also lost her eighteen-year-old son, Jack, the exact same way. On one horrifying night, two of Savage's four sons died of an opioid overdose. "It still haunts me," she says. "My husband and I have racked our brains over the hows and the whys. Why wouldn't they just say no?"[44]

"It is not enough to focus all our resources on treating people who are already addicted to opioids. Keeping people who do not have an opioid use disorder from becoming addicted is an equally important task."[43]

—Nora Volkow, director of NIDA

Savage wants other young people to "just say no." After taking a year to heal from their family's grief, she and her husband got a request from a community organization to speak at a parent event about substance abuse. They accepted and spoke to two hundred people about their family tragedy. "It was a wake-up call," says Savage. "It was a room filled with people who were terrified it could happen to them." After that night, schools started requesting that she come and speak to students, and she agreed. Now she travels to schools, conferences, and other events to tell her story. She is blunt in telling teens that "one little pill can kill somebody." She talks a lot about her sons, saying, "They were kids just like most of you. They were the smart kids . . . with bright futures who

Mike and Becky Savage lost their sons Nick and Jack to opioid overdose. Now they speak about their tragic story at schools, conferences, and other events in an effort to help young people understand how deadly opioid abuse is.

made a bad choice."[45] Savage is passionate about this work and cannot help wondering if her sons would still be alive if they really understood the risks of opioids—especially the danger of taking drugs without knowing who made them or where they came from.

The Savages also started a nonprofit called the 525 Foundation, which is named after her late sons' hockey numbers. The foundation provides information to parents and students about drugs, especially opioids, and encourages families to have open, honest conversations. Another endeavor of the foundation was initiating a local pill disposal program for unused opioid medications. Also, the Savages created a program called Wise-Up, which creates fact sheets on various substances that parents can use to initiate conversations with their children.

Prevention Through Accountability

Preventing opioid abuse can take many different forms, from educational programs and public awareness campaigns to government regulation. Another aspect of opioid abuse prevention is making doctors accountable when they overprescribe opioid medications. One of these doctors, Joel Smithers of Martinsville, Virginia, went far beyond overprescribing. He abused his medical license to prescribe opioids of all kinds to every single patient who visited his clinic—five hundred thousand doses in total. According to DEA agent Jesse Fong, Smithers flooded a region with opioid prescriptions and "hid behind his white doctor's coat as a large-scale drug dealer."

Investigators learned that word had traveled far and wide about Smithers's willingness to prescribe opioids to anyone who came to see him. People traveled to his clinic from neighboring states hundreds of miles away and sometimes waited twelve hours to see him. Upon receiving prescriptions for opioids, they either abused the drugs or sold them for profit. Smithers's illegal opioid operation finally came to an end, however. In October 2019 he was convicted of more than eight hundred counts of illegally prescribing opioids and was sentenced to forty years in prison.

Quoted in Adeel Hassan, "A Doctor Who Prescribed 500,000 Doses of Opioids Is Sent to Prison for 40 Years," *New York Times*, October 2, 2019. www.nytimes.com.

Operation Prevention

US government agencies are also getting involved with opioid abuse prevention, including the DEA. In partnership with Discovery Education, the DEA launched an opioid education initiative called Operation Prevention. The initiative is designed for middle and high school students, educators, and parents. The focus is on educating students about the science behind drug addiction and its impact, with educational resources designed to spark crucial conversations in the home and in the classroom. A DEA website about Operation Prevention explains, "This no-cost initiative will arm students with the tools they need to make smart, informed choices when they are prescribed or presented with the opportunity to experiment with opioids."[46]

A wide variety of materials is available through Operation Prevention, such as a collection of interactive student resources. The self-paced modules combine video, animation, and interactive elements, and they allow young people to "meet" teens who are struggling with prescription opioid abuse and heroin use and perhaps learn from their mistakes. By participating in virtual field trips, students get to know athletes and other professionals who have recovered from opioid addiction and now use their experience to help young people make smart choices. Other resources include educator lesson plans and parent tool kits, with the latter intended to empower parents with knowledge and resources. They learn the warning signs of opioid abuse and what the signs mean and gain other valuable knowledge that can help them help their children.

One element of the prevention program that is especially exciting for young people is called the Operation Prevention Video Challenge. Teens are invited to submit thirty- to sixty-second video public service announcements that communicate the opioid epidemic as a national crisis. In May 2019 four students from Coffee County Central High School in Manchester, Tennessee, won the year's grand prize in the video challenge and received $10,000 for their creation.

The students' powerful video, titled *What Could've Been*, is narrated by a teenage boy (one of the students) who is shown lying in the grass, musing about his life. He talks about his first car, about studying hard in school, graduating at the top of his class, and getting a full scholarship to college. He shares how he met the girl of his dreams, started a family, and grew old. Then what he reveals is a bit shocking—none of these things actually happened because the boy died from an opioid overdose. In a congratulatory message to the winners of the video challenge, the

DEA's Sean Fearns refers to the video as a "gripping video message that illustrates the gravity of opioid addiction and how it can devastate lives." Fearns emphasizes the value and importance of peer-to-peer influence in preventing opioid abuse before it starts. "We are truly encouraged by the leadership we've seen exhibited by our nation's youth,"[47] he says.

Critical Opioid Education

Because of how crucial preventing opioid abuse is in the United States, many other endeavors to reach young people have been implemented. In West Virginia, for example, Attorney General Patrick Morrisey has made it his mission to educate high school students about the dangers of opioid abuse. The state has been devastated by opioid overdose deaths. In 2017 there were 833 opioid-related overdose deaths in West Virginia, which was double the 2010 amount and three times the national rate of 14.6 deaths per 100,000 persons. Morrisey has taken aggressive action to develop and implement prevention efforts targeted at young people.

One of Morrisey's programs, which was launched in 2016, focuses on high school athletes. The initiative was sparked by a disturbing finding the previous year by researchers from New York University. In one of the first national studies of its kind, the researchers found that three-quarters of high school students who used heroin started by taking prescription opioid painkillers. Morrisey decided to use this information to educate young athletes because many of those who get injured while playing sports are prescribed opioids for pain. Thus, they have a higher risk for becoming addicted to opioids. The initiative aims to educate students, coaches, school officials, parents, and fans about the dangers of opioid abuse. An important part of this initiative is increasing awareness of nonopioid pain management for sports injuries, including physical therapy, nonopioid pain medications, acupuncture, and massage therapy, among others.

West Virginia has been devastated by opioid overdose deaths. In an effort to stop kids from dying, the state's attorney general, Patrick Morrisey (pictured), has made it his personal mission to educate high school students about the dangers of opioid abuse.

One tactic of the prevention initiative is designating athletic events as the Opioid Prevention Game of the Week. From 2016, when the initiative was first put into place, to the fall of 2019, 209 football games had received the game of the week designation, which has helped increase awareness of opioid dangers. Other efforts of the initiative include displaying and distributing educational materials in schools and staffing information booths at select sporting events to hand out opioid abuse educational materials.

All in all, the West Virginia prevention initiative has increased awareness of the risks involved with opioids and has proved to be

An important part of opioid abuse prevention among teens is promoting nonopioid pain management for sports injuries, rather than prescription opioid painkillers.

a catalyst for discussion of the issue. Morrisey shares his thoughts: "The success of this initiative shows the value of taking every opportunity possible to educate people about the dangers of opioid abuse."[48]

A Troubled State Digs In

Like West Virginia, Ohio has suffered terribly because of the opioid epidemic; it has one of the highest opioid overdose rates in the United States. This has spurred Ohio's governor, Mike DeWine, to take aggressive action in putting a multifaceted prevention program in place. One tactic was setting up the Ohio Opioid Education Alliance in 2018. This is a consortium of more than sixty organizations, including trade groups, corporations, and small businesses. As of 2019 the alliance had raised $5 million to fund a variety of prevention initiatives, one of which is an advertising campaign to educate Ohio citizens about the risks of opioids and how they can get help for addiction.

The ad campaign, which launched in June 2018, has a provocative title: Don't Live in Denial, Ohio. It introduced the public to the fictional town of Denial, Ohio, where parents do not believe their kids could be affected by the state's opioid crisis—in other words, they are in denial. The campaign uses multiple types of media, with a video on digital streaming platforms such as YouTube, Hulu, and Roku; television and radio ads; and billboards. There is also a website that offers a wide variety of information to educate people about the dangers of opioids. "Every child, every teen, is a potential victim of this epidemic," says Jonathan Wylly, chief fiscal officer for the Alcohol, Drug and Mental Health Board of Franklin County, Ohio. "Our plea is simple: Please, parents, don't live in Denial, Ohio."[49]

A 2019 survey showed that the Don't Live in Denial, Ohio, campaign has increased awareness of the opioid problem. The survey, which involved one thousand Ohio adult residents, found that nearly half of parents in central Ohio and about one-fourth of parents in other parts of the state had seen the ad campaign. Another finding was that more than half of parents had talked with their kids about the dangers of prescription opioids. But the survey also had some troubling findings and revealed there is still work to be done. More than 66 percent of parents and caregivers said they do not believe opioids are much of a problem in their local communities. After the survey results were compiled, health officials expressed concern that many parents in Ohio were indeed in denial of the opioid problem and seemed to think it was someone else's problem—nothing they needed to worry about.

> **"Every child, every teen, is a potential victim of this epidemic."[49]**
>
> —Jonathan Wylly, chief fiscal officer for the Alcohol, Drug and Mental Health Board of Franklin County, Ohio

Project H.O.P.E.

Another state that has suffered because of the opioid crisis is Pennsylvania. In January 2018 Pennsylvania governor Tom Wolf declared the state's heroin and opioid epidemic to be a statewide disaster emergency. Many preventive efforts have been initiated since that time, such as Heroin and Opioid Prevention Education, or H.O.P.E. This innovative program was developed in response to the severe problem of opioid abuse in Lehigh County, Pennsylvania, as well as other communities in the state. By participating in the H.O.P.E. program, students, teachers, and administrators

Pharmacies Help Prevent Opioid Abuse

As the federal government, state governments, communities, and schools enact programs that prevent opioid abuse, two major pharmacy chains are also getting involved. To make it easier for people to get rid of leftover prescription drugs—and in the process, prevent those drugs from being abused—Walgreens and CVS Health are beefing up their drug disposal programs. Both are installing kiosks in hundreds of their branch pharmacies and letting the public know what the kiosks are for.

Increasing awareness is important because under past federal law, pharmacies were not allowed to take back prescription medications. In order to get rid of unwanted drugs, people had to take them to police departments, which many did not want to do. The law was changed in 2014, and both CVS and Walgreens are working to get the word out. "We know firsthand patients are looking for solutions," says Rick Gates, Walgreens senior vice president of pharmacy operations. "We asked patients, and what we heard was bringing medications back to pharmacies felt like the right thing to do because they're the places they go to pick up their prescriptions." Walgreens started adding drug disposal kiosks in 2016 and within two years had collected more than 270 tons (245 metric tons) of medications. CVS also has disposal units throughout the United States and as of 2018 had collected 239 tons (217 metric tons) of medications.

Quoted in Angelica LaVito, "Drugstores Are Making It Easier to Empty Your Medicine Cabinet," CNBC, April 26, 2018. www.cnbc.com.

gain awareness and understanding. They learn what opioids are; the signs and symptoms of someone who is using (and/or abusing) opioids; the effects of opioid use on health, relationships, and life; and where to go for help.

The H.O.P.E. initiative has proved to be so effective in Pennsylvania that other states have adopted it, including Alaska, Oregon, and Ohio. One town in Ohio where the program is now in place is Belpre. School officials implemented the H.O.P.E. program after a high school athlete died from a heroin overdose the summer before his senior year. His death was hard on the students as well as teachers and administrators. "To lose a kid to anything is tragic," says former school superintendent Tony Dunn. "To lose a kid to something as preventable as an overdose, an accidental overdose, is devastating."[50]

A Formidable Task

There are no simple solutions to the opioid crisis in the United States. The problem is massive, affecting all fifty states and myriad communities nationwide, with tens of thousands of overdose deaths each year. And despite the many prevention efforts that have been implemented, there are no guarantees that they will make a significant difference. Still, health officials, government representatives, educators, community leaders, and medical professionals refuse to give up—saving lives is too important. With greater attention to increasing public awareness and helping the public understand that opioid abuse can affect anyone, anywhere, perhaps the time will come when these drugs are no longer the prevalent killers they are today.

Introduction: When Medicine Kills

1. Quoted in Steven Reinberg, "Overdose Deaths from Fentan-yl Soaring: Report," Consumer HealthDay, March 21, 2019. https://consumer.healthday.com.
2. Quoted in Benjamin Romano and Brendan Kiley, "'Fentanyl Is a Death Drug': Public-Health Warning Issued After Pills Kill 3 Local Teens," *Seattle Times*, October 7, 2019. www.seattle times.com.
3. Daniel Ciccarone, "Streets of Pain," Medium, June 13, 2018. https://medium.com.

Chapter One: A Growing Health Crisis

4. Ciccarone, "Streets of Pain."
5. Brynn Holland, "7 of the Most Outrageous Medical Treatments in History," History.com, April 1, 2019. www.history.com.
6. Jane Porter and Hershel Jick, "Addiction Rare in Patients Treated with Narcotics," letter to the editor, *New England Journal of Medicine*, January 10, 1980. www.nejm.org.
7. Ciccarone, "Streets of Pain."
8. Quoted in Dennis Thompson, "Fentanyl-Laced Crack Co-caine a Deadly New Threat," Consumer HealthDay, October 31, 2018. https://consumer.healthday.com.
9. Quoted in Dave Davies, "Deadly Fentanyl Bought Online from China Being Shipped Through the Mail," CBS News, Sep-tember 4, 2019. www.cbsnews.com.
10. Quoted in Linda Carroll, "Teens Still Commonly Prescribed Opioids, Study Finds," NBC News, May 28, 2019. www.nbc news.com.
11. Quoted in Kate Vidinsky, "Opioid Crisis: This Doctor's Street-Level Views Could Change the Course of the Epidemic," University of California, San Francisco, June 12, 2018. www .ucsf.edu/news.

Chapter Two: Highly Addictive Drugs

12. Quoted in FBI, "Chasing the Dragon: The Life of an Opiate Addict," February 4, 2016. www.fbi.gov.
13. Quoted in Centers for Disease Control and Prevention, "Cortney," September 22, 2017. www.cdc.gov.
14. Quoted in Centers for Disease Control and Prevention, "Cortney."
15. Quoted in Centers for Disease Control and Prevention, "Cortney."
16. Quoted in Rumsey Taylor, "Heroin Addiction Explained: How Opioids Hijack the Brain," *New York Times*, December 18, 2018. www.nytimes.com.
17. Quoted in Nina Bai and Dana Smith, "Body's 'Natural Opioids' Affect Brain Cells Much Differently than Morphine," University of California, San Francisco, May 10, 2018. www.ucsf.edu.
18. Quoted in Bai and Smith, "Body's 'Natural Opioids' Affect Brain Cells Much Differently than Morphine."
19. Quoted in Michael O. Schroeder, "Parents: Get Inside Your Adolescent's Brain to Prevent Addiction," *U.S. News & World Report*, September 28, 2017. https://health.usnews.com.
20. Nora Volkow, "Brain in Progress: Why Teens Can't Always Resist Temptation," *Nora's Blog*, National Institute on Drug Abuse, January 27, 2015. www.drugabuse.gov.
21. Mayo Clinic, "How Opioid Addiction Occurs," February 16, 2018. www.mayoclinic.org.
22. Quoted in Brad Schmitt, "Opioid Czar: Former Pill Abuser Now Battles Drug Epidemic in Tennessee," *Tennessean* (Nashville), September 1, 2017. www.tennessean.com.
23. Quoted in Schmitt, "Opioid Czar."

Chapter Three: The High Risks of Opioid Abuse

24. Quoted in Camille Bains, "Many Overdose Survivors Live with Brain Damage Doctors Still Don't Understand," HuffPost, December 31, 2018. www.huffingtonpost.ca.

25. National Institute on Drug Abuse, "Prescription Opioids," 2019. www.drugabuse.gov.
26. Quoted in Katharine Q. Seelye, "A Mother Lifts Her Son, Slowly, from Heroin's Abyss," *New York Times*, August 10, 2014. www.nytimes.com.
27. Quoted in Martha Bebinger, "What Doesn't Kill You Can Maim: Unexpected Injuries from Opioids," NPR, April 13, 2017. www.npr.org.
28. Quoted in Bebinger, "What Doesn't Kill You Can Maim."
29. Quoted in Davies, "Deadly Fentanyl Bought Online from China Being Shipped Through the Mail."
30. Ciccarone, "Streets of Pain."

Chapter Four: Treatment and Recovery Challenges

31. Richard Ries and Andrew J. Saxon, "Most People with Opioid Addictions Don't Get the Right Treatment: Medication-Assisted Therapy," STAT, September 21, 2017. www.statnews.com.
32. Quoted in Jessica Colarossi, "No Rx Required? Faster Access to Opioid-Based Medication Could Save Lives," The Brink, July 11, 2019. www.bu.edu.
33. Quoted in Jan Hoffman, "Most Doctors Are Ill-Equipped to Deal with the Opioid Epidemic. Few Medical Schools Teach Addiction," *New York Times*, September 10, 2018. www.nytimes.com.
34. Sarah Wakeman and Gary Mendell, "Follow the Evidence to Treat Opioid Addiction," STAT, January 22, 2018. www.statnews.com.
35. Quoted in German Lopez, "She Spent More than $110,000 on Drug Rehab. Her Son Still Died," Vox, September 3, 2019. www.vox.com.
36. Lopez, "She Spent More than $110,000 on Drug Rehab."
37. Nora Volkow, "What Does It Mean When We Call Addiction a Brain Disorder?," *Nora's Blog*, National Institute on Drug Abuse, March 23, 2018. www.drugabuse.gov.

38. Quoted in *Health Feed Blog*, University of Utah, "Fighting Fire with Fire: Taking on Opioid Addiction," August 13, 2019. https://healthcare.utah.edu.

39. Quoted in Colarossi, "No Rx Required?"

40. Quoted in Colarossi, "No Rx Required?"

41. Quoted in Christina Vogt, "Teens, Young Adults with Opioid Addiction Need Greater Access to Medication," Consultant 360, November 2018. www.consultant360.com.

42. Quoted in Vogt, "Teens, Young Adults with Opioid Addiction Need Greater Access to Medication."

Chapter Five: The Fight to Prevent Opioid Abuse

43. Nora Volkow, "The Importance of Prevention in Addressing the Opioid Crisis," *Nora's Blog*, National Institute on Drug Abuse, June 27, 2019. www.drugabuse.gov.

44. Quoted in Kate Thayer, "'Kids Just Like Most of You': Mother Who Lost 2 Sons on the Same Day Warns Students, Parents About Alcohol and Opioids," *Chicago Tribune*, May 2, 2019. www.chicagotribune.com.

45. Quoted in Thayer, "'Kids Just Like Most of You.'"

46. Drug Enforcement Administration, "Operation Prevention," Get Smart About Drugs, November 18, 2019. www.getsmart aboutdrugs.gov.

47. Quoted in Discovery Education, "The Drug Enforcement Administration, DEA Educational Foundation, and Discovery Education Announce Winners for 2019 'Operation Prevention' Video Challenge," May 9, 2019. www.discoveryeducation .com.

48. Quoted in West Virginia Attorney General's Office, "Opioid Abuse Prevention Initiative Surpasses 200 Football Games," *Beckley (WV) Register-Herald*, November 19, 2019. www .register-herald.com.

49. Quoted in Rita Price, "New Ads Warn, 'Don't Live in Denial, Ohio; Talk to Your Kids About Opioids,'" *Columbus (OH) Dispatch*, June 19, 2018. www.dispatch.com.

50. Quoted in Aaron Payne, "Opioid High: Students Face a Different Kind of Test," WOUB Public Media, September 10, 2016. https://woub.org.

ORGANIZATIONS AND WEBSITES

American Society of Addiction Medicine (ASAM)
—www.asam.org

ASAM seeks to improve the quality of addiction treatment, increase access to it, and support research and prevention efforts. Its website offers articles, fact sheets, and other publications about opioid abuse and addiction.

Centers for Disease Control and Prevention (CDC)
—www.cdc.gov

The CDC, which is the United States' leading health protection agency, seeks to control disease, injury, and disability. Numerous articles, fact sheets, and policy statements about opioids can be found on its website.

Drug Enforcement Administration (DEA)—www.dea.gov

The DEA is the United States' top drug law enforcement agency. Its website links to a separate site called Just Think Twice (www.justthinktwice.gov) that is designed for teenagers. A good collection of information about opioids can be found on the site, including real-life student addiction stories, fact sheets, news articles, and much more.

Foundation for a Drug-Free World—www.drugfreeworld.org

Foundation for a Drug-Free World seeks to empower young people with factual information about drugs so they can make smart decisions and live drug free. Its website offers a wealth of information about the dangers and risks associated with opioid abuse. Its personal testimonial videos are especially eye-opening.

I Am Not Anonymous—www.iamnotanonymous.org

I Am Not Anonymous seeks to end the stigma associated with addiction, spread awareness of addiction as a disease (rather than a moral failing), and help the millions of people who remain untreated

70

by sharing stories of hope. The website features a number of powerful stories of addicts who have turned their lives around.

National Institute on Drug Abuse (NIDA)—www.drugabuse.gov

NIDA seeks to advance research on the causes and effects of drug use and addiction and to apply that knowledge to improve public health. Its website links to a separate NIDA for Teens site (https://teens.drugabuse.gov/teens) that is designed for young people and provides a wealth of information about opioid abuse and addiction.

Partnership for Drug-Free Kids—https://drugfree.org

The Partnership for Drug-Free Kids is dedicated to supporting families who are addressing substance abuse and addiction. Its website's special Opioid Epidemic section offers valuable information about opioids, the risks involved with using them, and treatment options.

Substance Abuse and Mental Health Services Administration (SAMHSA)—www.samhsa.gov

SAMHSA seeks to reduce the impact of substance abuse on America's communities. The website's search engine produces numerous articles, fact sheets, and infographics on opioid abuse and addiction.

FOR FURTHER RESEARCH

Books

John Allen, *The Opioid Crisis*. San Diego, CA: ReferencePoint, 2020.

Sabine Cherenfant, ed., *The Opioid Crisis*. Farmington Hills, MI: Greenhaven, 2019.

Elisa Dawn Fortise Christensen, *The Fentanyl Warrior: How I Got Off and Stayed Off Opiates*. Seattle: Amazon Digital Services, 2019. Kindle edition.

Beth Macy, *Dopesick: Dealers, Doctors, and the Drug Company That Addicted America*. New York: Back Bay, 2019.

Jennifer Skancke, *Addicted to Opioids*. San Diego, CA: Reference-Point, 2020.

Ben Westhoff, *Fentanyl, Inc.: How Rogue Chemists Are Creating the Deadliest Wave of the Opioid Epidemic*. New York: Atlantic Monthly Press, 2019.

Christine Wilcox, *Opioid Abuse*. San Diego, CA: ReferencePoint, 2019.

Internet Sources

Addiction Center, "Fentanyl Addiction, Abuse and Treatment," 2019. www.addictioncenter.com.

American Society of Anesthesiologists, "Opioid Abuse." www.asahq.org.

Lenny Bernstein, "Deep Brain Stimulation Is Being Tested to Treat Opioid Addiction," *Washington Post*, November 6, 2019. www.washingtonpost.com.

Blake Dodge, "Drug Companies Aren't Apologizing for Their Role in the Opioid Crisis, Billions of Dollars in Settlements or Not," *Newsweek*, October 23, 2019. www.newsweek.com.

Gaby Galvin, "The Opioid Crisis Has Affected More than 2 Million Children," *U.S. News & World Report*, November 13, 2019. www.usnews.com.

Melissa Healy, "Who's to Blame for the Nation's Opioid Crisis? Massive Trial May Answer That Question," *Los Angeles Times*, September 18, 2019. www.latimes.com.

Mitchell S. Jackson, "The 'I Do' of Addiction," *New Yorker*, March 4, 2019. www.newyorker.com.

Lakeview Behavioral Health, "Opiates Abuse Causes, Addiction Signs, Symptoms & Side Effects," 2019. www.lakeviewbehavioralhealth.com.

Casey Leins, "Washington Tackles Opioid Use Disorder in Its Jails," *U.S. News & World Report*, October 25, 2019. www.usnews.com.

National Institute on Drug Abuse, "What Is Fentanyl?," 2019. www.drugabuse.gov.

National Institute on Drug Abuse for Teens, "Prescription Pain Medications (Opioids)," November 12, 2019. https://teens.drugabuse.gov.

Sam Quinones, "Physicians Get Addicted Too," *Atlantic*, May 2019. www.theatlantic.com.

Selena Simmons-Duffin, "The Real Cost of the Opioid Epidemic: An Estimated $179 Billion in Just 1 Year," *All Things Considered*, NPR, October 24, 2019. www.npr.org.

Dennis Thompson, "One Region Is Being Hit Hardest by Opioid Crisis," WebMD, 2019. www.webmd.com.

US Department of Health and Human Services, "Opioids and Adolescents," May 13, 2019. www.hhs.gov.

INDEX

ABOUT THE AUTHOR

Peggy J. Parks has written more than 150 educational books on a wide variety of topics for students of all ages. She holds a bachelor's degree from Aquinas College in Grand Rapids, Michigan, where she graduated magna cum laude. Parks lives in Muskegon, Michigan, a town she says inspires her writing because of its location on the shores of beautiful Lake Michigan.